SHERLOCK HOLMES
AND THE SPORT OF KINGS

Detectives must see, hear, and remember everything. They must be interested in the weather, people's shoes, flowers in a woman's hat, a box of matches in a man's pocket. They must understand people; they must know about dogs, and sheep, and horses. They must even know about horseracing, the sport of kings . . .

When Silver Blaze, a famous racehorse, disappears, Sherlock Holmes and Dr Watson go down to his Dartmoor stables. Silver Blaze is the favourite for a big race in a week's time, and his owner, Mr Ross, is hoping to win this race. But first, he needs to find his horse. There is also a dead man in the case – John Straker, Silver Blaze's trainer. His wife found his body in the mud not far from the stables. And Inspector Gregory needs to find the killer. But he and Mr Ross are getting the wrong answers to their questions.

So, says Sherlock Holmes, what *did* happen at the stables on Monday night? And, just as important, what did *not* happen?

OXFORD BOOKWORMS LIBRARY

Crime & Mystery

Sherlock Holmes and the Sport of Kings

Stage 1 (400 headwords)

Series Editor: Jennifer Bassett
Founder Editor: Tricia Hedge
Activities Editors: Jennifer Bassett and Christine Lindop

SIR ARTHUR CONAN DOYLE

Sherlock Holmes
and the
Sport of Kings

Retold by
Jennifer Bassett

Illustrated by
Ron Tiner

OXFORD UNIVERSITY PRESS

OXFORD
UNIVERSITY PRESS

Great Clarendon Street, Oxford OX2 6DP

Oxford University Press is a department of the University of Oxford.
It furthers the University's objective of excellence in research, scholarship,
and education by publishing worldwide in

Oxford New York

Auckland Cape Town Dar es Salaam Hong Kong Karachi
Kuala Lumpur Madrid Melbourne Mexico City Nairobi
New Delhi Shanghai Taipei Toronto

With offices in

Argentina Austria Brazil Chile Czech Republic France Greece
Guatemala Hungary Italy Japan Poland Portugal Singapore
South Korea Switzerland Thailand Turkey Ukraine Vietnam

OXFORD and OXFORD ENGLISH are registered trade marks of
Oxford University Press in the UK and in certain other countries

This simplified edition © Oxford University Press 2008

Database right Oxford University Press (maker)

First published in Oxford Bookworms 2003

18 20 19

The original version of this story was published under the title *Silver Blaze*

ISBN 978 0 19 478920 2

A complete recording of this Bookworms edition of
Sherlock Holmes and the Sport of Kings is available.

Printed in China

Word count (main text): 5925 words

For more information on the Oxford Bookworms Library,
visit www.oup.com/elt/gradedreaders

CONTENTS

1
A horse called Silver Blaze

'I must go down there, Watson. I must,' said Sherlock Holmes at the breakfast table on Thursday morning.

'Go? Go where?' I asked.

'To Dartmoor – to King's Pyland.'

'Ah! So that's it,' I said. 'Well, everybody in the country is talking about the case at King's Pyland.'

I always know when Holmes is interested in a case. He reads all the newspapers, he walks up and down, up and down the room, and does not speak for hours.

He did all those things yesterday. He did not answer any of my questions, but I knew that it was the mystery at King's Pyland.

The morning newspapers were on the breakfast table. 'What is happening at King's Pyland? Where is Silver Blaze?' they asked. 'Who killed John Straker? What are the police doing? Can they find the horse before the big race next week?'

Silver Blaze was a famous racehorse, and John Straker was his trainer. One of the biggest horse races of the year – the Wessex Cup – was next week, and Silver Blaze was the favourite to win. But on Monday night at King's

1

'Where is Silver Blaze?' the newspapers asked.

2

Pyland two things happened. Someone killed John Straker, and Silver Blaze disappeared.

I was interested in this case too. 'Do you need my help, Holmes?' I asked. 'I would very much like to come with you.'

'My dear Watson,' said Holmes, 'of course you must come with me. We can catch the twelve o'clock from Paddington, and talk about the case on the train.'

Two hours later we were on the train to Tavistock. We read all the midday newspapers, but there was nothing new in them.

'So, Watson, what do you think about this case?'

'Well, the newspapers say—'

'Ah, yes. The newspapers understand nothing. One day they say one thing, the next day they say another. But we must look at the case more carefully. What *did* happen on Monday night at King's Pyland? And what did *not* happen? That's an important question too.'

'Do the police have any answers?' I asked.

'No,' said Holmes. 'On Wednesday morning I had two letters. One was from Mr Ross, the owner of the horse, and the other was from the Dartmoor police – an Inspector Gregory. They ask for my help.'

'Wednesday morning!' I cried. 'But this is Thursday morning. Why didn't you go down yesterday?'

'Because it was an easy case. You can't hide a famous

3

horse for long, I thought. Where can you hide a horse on Dartmoor? There are no buildings, no trees . . . But I was wrong, Watson. The case is now two days old, and nobody can find the horse – or Straker's killer. So here we are, on the train to Tavistock.'

'And what do you think about it all?' I said.

'Well, Watson, let's look at the case. First, we have a racehorse, Silver Blaze – only five years old, but already a winner in many big races. His owner, Mr Ross, is a happy man – and rich. The racegoers are happy too. Silver Blaze nearly always wins his races, and so people put big bets on him to win. And when the favourite wins the race, a lot of people make money on their bets. But what happens when the favourite *doesn't* win, Watson? What then?'

'A lot of people lose their money, of course,' I said. 'And people with big bets on a *different* horse can make much *more* money, when that other horse wins.'

'Right, Watson! So perhaps some people are very interested in Silver Blaze *not* running in the Wessex Cup. Of course, Mr Ross and his trainer, John Straker, know that, and they watch the horse very carefully.

'Now, let's look at the people and the place. The trainer, John Straker – a good man and wonderful with horses – worked for Mr Ross for twelve years. There are four horses in the training stables, and three boys

*There are four horses in the training stables,
and three boys working for Straker.*

working for Straker. One of them sits up all night with the horses, and the other two sleep in a room over the stables. We know nothing bad about any of the boys.

'Straker has a wife, no children, and lives – I mean, lived – in a house about two hundred metres from the stables. The town of Tavistock is two kilometres to the west, and about two kilometres to the east there is Capleton, another training stables. The owner there is Lord Backwater, and the trainer is Silas Brown. There are no other houses – just the hills of Dartmoor.'

I listened carefully. I wanted to remember it all because Holmes does not like to say anything twice.

'Now,' he said, 'what happened on Monday night? These papers came with Inspector Gregory's letter. The best thing is for you to read them, Watson. Then tell me what you think.'

I took the papers from him, and began to read.

2
Monday night at King's Pyland

Notes by Inspector Gregory, after talking to Edith Baxter, Ned Hunter, Mrs John Straker, and Mr Fitzroy Simpson

On Monday evening Straker locked the stables at nine o'clock, the usual time. Two of the boys then walked up to the trainer's house for their dinner, but the third boy, Ned Hunter, stayed in the stables to watch the horses. At five past nine, the Strakers' servant, a girl called Edith Baxter, carried Ned Hunter's dinner down to the stables. The dinner that night was a hot meat curry.

Edith was nearly at the stables when a man called out to her. He came up to her, and she saw a tall man in a grey suit and a hat, and a red and black scarf. He carried a big walking stick, and Edith felt afraid of him.

'Where am I?' the man asked. 'What is this place?'

'This is King's Pyland training stables,' she said.

'Good!' said the man. 'Now, a stable boy sleeps here every night – is that right? And I think you're taking his dinner to him now.' He took an envelope out of his pocket. 'Please give the boy this, and you can have some money for a beautiful new dress.'

Edith did not take the envelope. She ran past the man to the stables and up to a small open window. She always put the boy's dinner through this window, and Ned Hunter was there, ready to take it.

'Oh Ned!' Edith cried, but before she could say any more, the stranger came up behind her.

Edith ran past the man to the stables.

'Good evening,' he said through the window to the boy. 'I want to talk to you.'

'Who are you? What do you want?' Ned Hunter said.

'I want to make you rich, boy,' the stranger said. 'You help me, and I help you. You have two horses in for the Wessex Cup – Silver Blaze and Bayard. I hear that Bayard is the better horse, and that you stable boys are putting your bets on him to win. Am I right?'

'I'm not saying anything!' cried Ned Hunter. 'We don't talk about our horses at King's Pyland, so get out! I'm getting the dog now!'

Ned ran across the stables to get the dog, and Edith began to run back to the house. But she looked back after about thirty metres, and saw the man at the little window, with his head and one arm inside the room.

Edith ran on, and a minute later, Ned came out of the building and locked the door behind him. He ran all round the stables with the dog, but the man was gone.

Ned Hunter told the trainer and the other boys about the stranger, but no one saw him again.

The next thing happened at one o'clock in the morning when John Straker got out of bed.

'What's the matter?' said his wife. 'Where are you going?'

'To the stables,' Straker said. 'I can't stop thinking about that stranger. I just want to have a look around.'

'But it's raining. Wait until the rain stops,' she said.

'No, no,' Straker said. 'I want to go now.'

He left the house and Mrs Straker went back to sleep. At seven in the morning she woke up, but her husband was not there. She quickly got up, called the servant, Edith, and they ran down to the stables.

They found the stables unlocked. Straker was not there, and inside, on a chair, Ned Hunter slept like a dead man. Silver Blaze was gone, and his stable door was open. They called the other two boys from the room over the stables. They were good sleepers and heard nothing in the night.

Nobody could wake Ned Hunter, so the two women and the boys ran out to look for the trainer and the horse. Five hundred metres from the stables, they saw Straker's coat on a small tree. Down the hill, just past the tree, they found the trainer. He was dead.

There was a long cut in his leg, and his head was broken in three places. In his right hand he had a small knife, with blood all over it, and in his left hand he had a red and black scarf.

Edith Baxter knew the scarf at once, and later, so did Ned Hunter.

'It's the stranger's scarf,' he told us. 'When I went to get the dog, that stranger was still at the stable window. He put something in my meat curry, to make me sleep – I

Just past the tree, they found the trainer. He was dead.

know he did. Edith saw him, with his arm through the window.'

Ned Hunter was right about his meat curry. There was some of his dinner left, and we found a lot of opium in it. That's why Ned slept like a dead man.

What about the horse? We found his tracks in the mud,

next to Straker's dead body. But what happened then? Someone hit Straker on the head, and killed him. Did that person take the horse away? Did the horse run away? Everybody on Dartmoor is looking for Silver Blaze, but there is no news of him.

When I began work on the case on Tuesday, we looked for the stranger. He was in Tavistock, and we found him easily. His name is Fitzroy Simpson. He lives mostly in London, and makes his money at the races, taking bets. We looked in his betting-book, and found a number of big bets – five thousand pounds – *against the favourite* for the Wessex Cup.

These were his answers to my questions.

'Why did you come down to Dartmoor?'

'I'm a betting man, Inspector. I need to know about the horses for the Wessex Cup – Silver Blaze, Bayard, and Desborough, the horse at Silas Brown's stables. He's the second favourite for the race, you see.'

'Did you go to the King's Pyland stables late on Monday evening?'

'Yes, I did. I just wanted to ask the stable boys some questions. They know the horses better than anyone.'

'And is this your scarf?'

'Yes . . . yes, it is.'

'And how did it get into the dead man's hand, Mr Simpson? Can you tell us that?'

'I don't know, Inspector, I don't know! I never saw the man. I lost my scarf in the dark. It wasn't me, Inspector, it wasn't me!'

We asked many more questions, but Fitzroy Simpson did not change his story. He was out at King's Pyland that night, his suit was still wet from the rain, and his big walking stick could break a man's head open. But there were no cuts on his body, so where did the blood on Straker's knife come from?

And where is the horse?

'It wasn't me, Inspector, it wasn't me!' said Fitzroy Simpson.

3
John Straker's pockets

'Mmm, very interesting,' I said. I gave the papers back to Holmes, and he put them away.

'So, Watson, what can you tell me?' he asked.

I thought for a minute. 'This cut on Straker's leg. Perhaps he did it with his own knife. When something hits you very hard on the head, and you have a knife in your hand . . . It can happen, you know.'

'Very good, Watson. And that's bad news for Fitzroy Simpson.'

'So did Simpson do it, do you think?' I said.

'Perhaps,' said Holmes. 'Let's look at it. Simpson puts opium in the boy's dinner. He goes away and comes back later in the night. He gets into the stables, takes the horse out, and leaves. But the trainer arrives at that moment, sees him, and follows him. The two men fight, and Simpson breaks Straker's head open with his stick. Then Simpson takes the horse – but where? Or did the horse run away? Is it still out on the moor? And how did Simpson get into the *locked* stables? I don't know, Watson, I don't know. We must wait and see.'

When we arrived at Tavistock station, two men came

to meet us. Inspector Gregory was a tall, slow-moving man with blue eyes, and Mr Ross was small and quick. He was the first to speak.

'Very pleased to see you, Mr Holmes. The Inspector here is working hard, but we need help. We must find poor Straker's killer, and I want to find my horse.'

'Is there any news?' asked Holmes.

'Let's talk on the way,' the Inspector said. 'I'd like you to see everything in the daylight.'

We were soon out of the little town and up on the brown hills of the moor.

We were soon up on the brown hills of the moor.

15

Inspector Gregory thought that the killer was Fitzroy Simpson. 'Simpson was out in the rain that night. His suit was still wet on the Tuesday,' he said. 'He had a big stick, and his scarf was in the dead man's hand. That looks bad, Mr Holmes, very bad.'

Holmes smiled. 'You need more than that, Inspector. The servant, Edith, spoke of an envelope. Did Simpson say anything about that?'

'Yes, he said it had money in it – a ten-pound note for the stable boy.'

'What about this other training stables, at Capleton?' asked Holmes. 'Does Simpson have friends there?'

'No, we don't think so. We went to Capleton, of course. Their horse, Desborough, is the second favourite for the Wessex Cup, and Silas Brown, the trainer, was not friendly with Straker. But we found nothing.'

When we arrived at King's Pyland, Inspector Gregory took us into the trainer's house.

'Straker's body is upstairs,' he said. 'But we have here the things from his pockets and from the ground next to his body. Would you like to see them, Mr Holmes?'

'Very much,' said Holmes.

We went into the front room, and the Inspector opened a box and put things on a table. There was a box of matches, a small piece of candle, some money, a watch, some papers, and a small, thin knife.

The Inspector opened a box and put things on a table.

'This is a strange knife,' Holmes said. He looked at it carefully, and then gave it to me. 'What is it, Watson?'

'It's an eye knife,' I said. 'Doctors use these when they cut into an eye. You don't usually see them outside a hospital.'

'Mm,' said Holmes. 'So why did Straker take this knife? It's no good for fighting.'

'His wife says it was in the bedroom for some days,' said Inspector Gregory. 'Perhaps he just took it because it was there on the table.'

'Perhaps,' said Holmes. 'What about these papers?'

'One is a letter from Mr Ross, the others are bills,' the Inspector said. 'Three of them are bills for the horses' food, and this one is a bill from a dress-maker in London, for a Mr William Darbyshire. He was a friend of Straker's, his wife tells us. His letters sometimes came here, and Straker sent them on.'

'Mrs William Darbyshire is an expensive lady,' said Holmes, looking at the bill. 'Twenty-five pounds is a lot of money, for just one dress and one hat.' He put the bill down and moved to the window. 'Inspector, can we go out on the moor now, before the light begins to go?'

We left the room and at the front door we saw a woman. She came up to Inspector Gregory and put her hand on his arm. 'Is there any news?' she said.

'No, Mrs Straker, but here is Mr Holmes, the famous detective from London. We have him to help us now.'

'I think I met you a month or two ago, Mrs Straker,' said Holmes. 'Let me see . . . Yes, it was in Plymouth, at a garden-party. Do you remember?'

'No, sir. That wasn't me.'

'But I remember so well . . . You had a blue dress, and a dark blue hat with white flowers on it.'

'I don't have a hat with flowers on it, sir,' Mrs Straker said.

'Well, well, I am wrong, then. I am so sorry.' And with that Holmes followed the Inspector outside. The four of

'It was in Plymouth, at a garden-party. Do you remember?'

us then walked past the stables and up onto the moor. After ten minutes Inspector Gregory stopped.

'Here we are,' he said. 'Straker's body was just down there. His coat was here, on this small tree—'

'On the tree? Not on the ground?' Holmes asked.

'Oh no. It was on the tree, carefully away from the mud on the ground.'

'Mmm. Interesting,' said Holmes. 'Now, I must look at the mud down there.'

'Ah,' said Inspector Gregory, 'and to help you, I have here in this bag one of Straker's shoes, one of Fitzroy Simpson's shoes, and one of Silver Blaze's horseshoes.'

'My dear Inspector, well done!' Holmes was very pleased. 'You think of everything.'

For some minutes Holmes looked carefully at the ground, his eyes only centimetres away from the mud.

'Hello!' he said suddenly. 'What's this?' From out of the mud he took a match, or a small piece of one.

'Now why didn't I find that?' said the Inspector.

'I knew it was there, you see,' said Holmes.

'You *knew*? But how could you know that?'

Holmes smiled but did not answer. He then took the shoes, got down on the ground, and began to look at all the tracks in the mud. We stood and watched him, but after five minutes Mr Ross looked at his watch.

'Er, this is very interesting, Mr Holmes,' he said, 'but is it going to take a long time?'

'No,' said Holmes. He got to his feet. 'I don't need to do any more here. Watson and I are going to take a little walk across the moor now, with the horseshoe.'

Mr Ross looked at the Inspector. 'Can we go back to the house and talk? I must take Silver Blaze's name out of the Wessex Cup race – and do it today, I think.'

'Don't do that!' cried Holmes. 'No, no, you must leave the horse's name in for the race.'

'But . . .' Mr Ross began. Then he laughed, a little angrily. 'Well, thank you, Mr Holmes. Thank you for your help. See you later then, at the house.'

And he and the Inspector walked away.

Holmes began to look at all the tracks in the mud.

21

4
Looking for a horse

Holmes and I walked slowly across the moor. In the evening sunlight the autumn colours on the hills were beautiful – reds and browns and yellows.

But Holmes saw nothing of that. 'So, Watson,' he said, 'let's forget John Straker for a minute, and think about the horse. Horses are friendly animals. Let's say that Silver Blaze runs away after the killing. Here he is, out on the cold wet moor. What does he do next?'

'He looks for a nice warm stable,' I said, 'with food and water.'

'Right, Watson. He didn't go back to King's Pyland, we know that, but there is another stable not far away, at Capleton. Perhaps he went there. And the way to Capleton, Watson, is down this hill. Let's go!'

We walked quickly down the hill, and at the bottom we found a small river and some very wet ground.

'Wonderful,' said Holmes. 'I wanted mud, and here it is. You follow the left side of the river, Watson. We're looking for the tracks of horseshoes.'

We found them after only fifty metres. Holmes took the horseshoe out of his pocket and put it next to the tracks. 'Yes, that's Silver Blaze, no question about it.'

We followed the tracks easily, then lost them for a time, but found them again about two hundred metres from the Capleton stables.

'Here they are,' I cried. 'And look – there's another track here, of a man's shoe.'

Holmes put the horseshoe next to the tracks.
'Yes, that's Silver Blaze.'

Holmes got down to look. 'You're right, Watson. And the man is walking next to the horse.'

We followed the two tracks to Capleton stables, and were still twenty metres away when a man came out and called to us. He had a red, angry face.

'Go away! We don't want visitors here! Go away!'

'Mr Silas Brown?' Holmes said to him.

'What do you want?' said the man. 'I don't talk to newspaper people, so just go away.'

'We are not from a newspaper,' said Holmes, smiling. 'But you have a horse called Silver Blaze in your stable.'

'That's not true!' Mr Brown said angrily.

'Shall we go in and talk about it?' said Holmes. He did not wait for an answer, but took the man's arm and moved quickly to the gate. He looked back at me and said quietly, 'Wait for me here, Watson.'

Twenty minutes later they came out again. Holmes looked pleased, and Mr Silas Brown was a different man. He looked smaller and older, and his face was afraid.

'Remember,' said Holmes, 'you must be there on the day, on time, and everything must be ready.'

'Yes, yes,' Silas Brown said quickly. 'You can be sure of it. Oh yes, you can be sure of it.'

'Good,' said Holmes. 'Well, goodbye for now.'

Holmes and I then began to walk back to King's Pyland along the road.

'Wait for me here, Watson,' Holmes said to me quietly.

'Does he have the horse, then?' I asked.

Holmes laughed. 'Yes. He said no at first, of course, but he's afraid of the police. He doesn't want them to know about this, and I can help him with that.'

'But why didn't the police find the horse?' I asked. 'Inspector Gregory said they went to Capleton.'

'Oh, it's easy to change the colour of a horse's coat.' Holmes laughed again. 'Gregory is a good policeman, but I don't think he knows much about horses.'

'And why did Brown tell *you*?' I said.

25

'When I walked through the stables with him,' said Holmes, 'the ground was muddy and I saw the tracks of his shoes in the mud. You remember those tracks on the moor? Well, these were the same shoes. After that, it was easy, and he told me everything. He found Silver Blaze on the moor early in the morning and brought him into the stables. The horse is very well, just a different colour at the moment. Brown put a very big bet on Desborough to win the Wessex Cup, you see. And with Silver Blaze out of the race . . .'

'But why did you leave the horse there? Is it safe with him?' I did not understand Holmes's plan.

'My dear Watson,' Holmes said, 'the horse is very safe. Silas Brown is afraid of me, afraid of the police, afraid of losing everything. Silver Blaze must be ready to race next week, or Brown's life as a racehorse trainer is finished – and Brown knows that.'

'Mr Ross isn't going to like it,' I said.

'Mr Ross', said Holmes, 'doesn't understand detective work. He wants answers today, now, at once. So, he must learn a lesson. He must learn to wait. Say nothing about Silver Blaze for the moment, Watson.'

Back at King's Pyland, we found Mr Ross and Inspector Gregory in the trainer's house.

'An interesting visit,' said Holmes. 'But my friend and I must go back to London by the midnight train.'

The Inspector and Mr Ross stared at him, and I saw that Holmes was right about Mr Ross.

'So our famous London detective can't find poor Straker's killer,' Mr Ross said. 'Or my horse.'

'It's a difficult case, that's true,' said Holmes quietly. 'But your horse is going to run in the Wessex Cup next Tuesday. You have my promise on that.'

'Hm! A promise is a wonderful thing,' said Mr Ross. 'But I would like the horse better than a promise.'

Holmes smiled, then turned to Inspector Gregory. 'Inspector, can you give me a photograph of Straker?'

'Yes, of course,' said the Inspector. He took one from an envelope in his pocket and gave it to Holmes.

It was now time to go back to Tavistock, and we went outside. One of the stable boys was there, and Holmes suddenly spoke to him.

'I see you have some sheep here, next to the stables,' he said. 'Are they all well?'

'They're all right, sir,' said the boy, 'but two or three of them are a little lame. They went lame last week.'

Holmes was very pleased about this. He got into the carriage and said to the Inspector, 'Remember the lame sheep, Gregory, remember the lame sheep!'

Mr Ross was not interested in the sheep, but the Inspector stared at Holmes. 'You think the sheep are important?'

'Two or three of the sheep are a little lame,' said the boy.

'Oh yes,' said Holmes. 'Very important.'

The Inspector still stared at him, very interested now. 'And what other things are important, Mr Holmes?'

'The strange incident of the dog in the night-time.'

'The dog did nothing in the night-time.'

'That was the strange incident.'

5
A day at the races

On Tuesday Holmes and I took the train to Winchester, and Mr Ross met us at the station. He drove us to the races, but he was not a happy man.

'Well, Mr Holmes,' he said coldly. 'Do you have news of my horse?'

Holmes smiled. 'He's safe and well, I'm sure. How is the betting for the Wessex Cup?'

'Very strange,' said Mr Ross. 'Yesterday Silver Blaze was fifteen to one, but today he's the favourite, at three to one. Why, I don't know.'

'Ah!' said Holmes. 'Somebody knows something!'

We arrived only minutes before the beginning of the Wessex Cup race. This was Holmes's plan, I think. Mr Ross had no time to ask questions. There were six horses running in the race, and Silver Blaze's name was there, at number 4. The horses began to come out for the race, and Mr Ross got very excited.

'Where is he? I can't see him!' he cried.

'There are two more horses to come out,' I said. 'And look! There's number 4 now, in racing colours of red and blue. Those are your colours, Mr Ross.'

Silver Blaze came past us, looking strong and well.

And there was Silver Blaze, a big brown horse with a white nose. He came past us, looking strong and well, and ready for anything.

'Holmes,' cried Mr Ross, 'I was wrong about you! I'm sorry. But why, how—?'

'Shh!' said Holmes. 'Watch! Yes, they're off!'

It was a good race, fast and exciting. After the first minute, a horse with yellow racing colours came to the front, and stayed there.

'That's Desborough, from the Capleton stables,' said Holmes. 'A good horse, but Silver Blaze is better.'

But Silver Blaze was three horses behind Desborough.

'Come on, come on!' cried Mr Ross. 'Move up now!'

We all watched the red and blue colours. 'Yes!' I said. 'Look, he's moving up now! Watch him go!'

Slowly but surely, Silver Blaze moved up into fourth place, then into third place, then into second place. Now only Desborough was in front of him.

'That's my boy!' said Mr Ross. 'Go on, go on!'

'Desborough's getting tired,' Holmes said. 'Watch!'

Eighty metres, fifty metres . . . 'He's away!' cried Mr Ross. 'His nose is in front, yes, yes, he's going to do it!'

And he did. Silver Blaze kept his nose in front, finished first, and won the Wessex Cup.

'Wonderful!' said Mr Ross. 'Wonderful! What a race! What a horse! Mr Holmes, how can I thank you?'

'You must thank the horse, not me,' said Holmes, smiling. 'Let's go down and have a look at him.'

Silver Blaze was still excited by his big race. Mr Ross looked him up and down. 'He looks well, very well. I

'His nose is in front, yes, yes, he's going to do it!'

don't understand any of it, Mr Holmes. How did you do it? Where did you find him? And perhaps you now have John Straker's killer too. Do you?'

'Yes,' said Holmes quietly. 'Yes, I have him too.'

Mr Ross and I stared at him. 'You have him?' Mr Ross said. 'Where is he?'

'He is here.'

'Here! Where?'

'Here with me now, at this moment.'

Mr Ross's face began to go red. 'What are you saying, Mr Holmes?' he said angrily. 'Are you saying—?'

Sherlock Holmes laughed. 'No, no, Mr Ross, not *you*. The killer is standing behind us.'

He turned and put his hand on Silver Blaze's back.

'The horse?' cried Mr Ross.

'The horse!' I said.

'Yes, the horse,' said Holmes. 'But don't be angry with him. You can hear all about the mystery, but later, please. I have a little bet on a horse in the next race, and I would like to see it win . . .'

6
Holmes has the answers

On the train back to London Holmes told us the story behind the mystery, and the time went very quickly.

'Before we went down to King's Pyland,' my friend began, 'I thought it was Fitzroy Simpson. But when we arrived at the stables, I suddenly remembered the hot meat curry. Why didn't I think of it before? That, you see, was the beginning.'

'The meat curry . . .' said Mr Ross, thinking about it. 'Er, how did the meat curry help you?'

'Do you know the taste of opium?' Holmes said. 'No? Well, it's not a very strong taste, but it's there. You can taste it in most food, but not in curry. Curry has a very strong taste, stronger than opium. So the killer says, "I need a night when the dinner is a meat curry. Then Ned Hunter can eat his dinner happily, without the taste of opium – and go to sleep." But did Fitzroy Simpson know that curry was the dinner on Monday night? Of course not. How could he? He didn't make the dinner, he was a stranger at King's Pyland, he knew nobody in the trainer's house. So, we forget Simpson, and think again. Who knew about the curry *before* dinner on that Monday night?'

On the train Holmes told us the story behind the mystery.

'John Straker and his wife,' I said. 'And the servant.'

'Right, Watson. And so on to the next question, about the dog. We know there was a dog in the stables that night because Ned Hunter took the dog out when Simpson was there. Then in the middle of the night someone went into the stables and took out a horse. The two boys sleeping upstairs in the stables heard nothing, because there was nothing to hear. The dog *did not bark*. Why not?'

'Aha!' said Mr Ross. 'It didn't bark, because it *knew* the visitor. Dogs only bark at strangers.'

'Right again. So, the midnight visitor was John Straker. But why did he take the horse out? What did he want? It was something dishonest, or why did he put opium in his stable boy's dinner? We all know about dishonest trainers. They can make a lot of money – they put big bets *against* their own horse, and then stop their horse winning. But how? What was Straker's plan here? Perhaps the answer was in his pockets, I thought.

'And so it was. You remember the strange knife? Dr Watson here told us about it – an eye knife, used by doctors in hospitals. With a knife like this, you can make a cut – a very, very small cut – in the tendon of a horse's back leg. Nobody can see the cut, and the horse only feels it a little. He's not lame, but he doesn't run his best, so he cannot win the race.'

'And Straker wanted to do *this* to my horse?' cried Mr Ross. 'How could he? I thought he was a good man!'

'No,' said Holmes. 'He wasn't a good man – or a careful one. No horse stands quietly when a knife goes into its back leg. Straker didn't want anyone to hear the noise, so he took the horse out onto the moor.'

'The candle, and the match,' I said. 'Of course!'

'That's right,' Holmes said. 'And I learnt more from Straker's pockets too. You are a man of the world, Mr Ross. Do men carry other men's bills around in their pockets? No, they do not. So who was Mr Darbyshire? Another name for John Straker. And there was a lady in the case, too. A very expensive lady. I talked to Mrs Straker about the dress and the hat on the bill, but she knew nothing about them.'

'And on Monday night, out on the moor,' said Mr Ross, 'what happened, do you think?'

'How about this?' said Holmes. 'Straker takes the horse down the hill. He sees Simpson's scarf on the ground, and takes it with him – why, I don't know. He puts his coat on a tree, gets out the candle and the matches, and the knife, and begins his work. But Silver Blaze doesn't like it. Perhaps he's afraid, perhaps he feels something is wrong. He's a big strong horse, and he gets angry. He kicks out with his back legs, and the horseshoes hit Straker on the head. Straker goes down,

Silver Blaze kicks out, and Straker goes down, into the mud.

into the mud, and the knife in his hand goes into his own leg. The horse disappears into the night.'

'Wonderful!' Mr Ross said. 'You tell it very well, Mr Holmes. I see it all now.'

'And the sheep?' I asked. 'What about the sheep? You told Inspector Gregory that they were important.'

'Ah yes, Watson, the sheep.' Holmes smiled. 'And they *were* important. It's not easy to make a very small cut in an animal's tendon, and Straker did not want to get it wrong. He needed to practise first, but what on? There were his own sheep, right in front of him.'

'And where did you go in London, the day after we got back?' I asked. 'Was it to that dress-maker on the bill for Mr Darbyshire?'

'Very good, Watson!' Holmes laughed. 'Yes, I had a photograph of Straker, and the dress-maker knew him at once. "Oh yes," she said, "that's Mr Darbyshire. I do a lot of work for him. Mrs Darbyshire is a very beautiful lady, and she likes expensive dresses."' Holmes laughed again. 'It's an old, old story. Straker is not the first man with two women in his life. He needed more money for the expensive Mrs Darbyshire, so he thought of this plan with Silver Blaze. And there you have it, Mr Ross.'

'Yes, I understand it all now,' said Mr Ross, 'and thank you very much, Mr Holmes. There's just one thing. Where was the horse?'

Straker needed more money for the expensive Mrs Darbyshire.

'Ah, yes. The horse was safe and well, and with a friend,' said Sherlock Holmes. 'I can't tell you who or where, because I made a promise. But here we are, nearly in London. You have the answer to the mystery, Mr Ross, you are the winner of the Wessex Cup, and the owner of the fastest racehorse in the south of England. What more do you need?'

GLOSSARY

bet *(n)*   when you risk money on the result of a race (if you are
   right, you win money; if you are wrong, you lose money)

bill   a piece of paper that shows how much money you must pay

blood   the red liquid inside your body

broken *(adj)*   in pieces; not working

candle   a piece of wax that burns to give light

case   a problem that the police must find an answer to

curry   meat or vegetables cooked with spices that taste hot

dear   a word that shows you like someone

disappear   to go away so people cannot see you

dishonest   saying things that are not true; doing bad things

envelope   a paper cover for a letter

favourite   in a race, the horse that you expect to win

fight *(v)*   to try to hurt or kill somebody

follow   to go or come after somebody or something

ground   the sky is over your head; the ground is under your feet

horse   a big animal that can carry people on its back

incident   something that happens

inspector   an important policeman

kick *(v)*   to hit somebody or something with your foot

lame   not able to walk well because of a bad leg or foot

lock (unlock) *(v)*   to close (open) a door with a key

matches   short thin pieces of wood that can make fire

moor   wild land on hills, with not many trees

mud   soft wet earth (**muddy**, covered with mud)

mystery   something strange that you cannot understand or
   explain

newspaper   you read a newspaper every day to find out what is
   happening in the world

opium a strong, dangerous drug that can make people sleep

own belonging to a person (e.g. I have my own room)

owner a person who has something

police a group of people whose job is to catch criminals

promise *(n)* when you say that you are certainly going to do (or not do) something

race *(n)* a competition to see which horse (car, etc.) is the fastest

racegoer a person who goes to horse races

safe not in danger

scarf a piece of material to wear round the neck

servant somebody who works in another person's house

sheep a farm animal, used for its wool and for meat

stable a building that a horse lives in

stare to look at somebody or something for a long time

stick *(n)* a long piece of wood

strange very unusual or surprising

stranger somebody that you do not know

strong a strong horse (or person) does not get tired easily; tastes and smells can also be strong (e.g. oranges)

sure when you are sure, you know that something is true

taste *(n)* the feeling that food gives in the mouth (e.g. sugar has a sweet taste)

tendon something in the body that joins a muscle to a bone

track *(n)* a mark that an animal's foot makes on the ground

trainer a person who teaches animals to do something

wet not dry; with water in it

win to be the first in a race or game

winner a person or animal that wins a race, game, etc.

Sherlock Holmes
and the Sport of Kings

ACTIVITIES

ACTIVITIES

Before Reading

1 Read the back cover of the book, and the introduction on the first page. How much do you know now about the story? Tick one box for each sentence.

	YES	NO
1 Silver Blaze is a racehorse.	☐	☐
2 Sherlock Holmes is the owner of Silver Blaze.	☐	☐
3 Racehorses make money when they win races.	☐	☐
4 Silver Blaze's trainer is dead.	☐	☐
5 Mr Ross found John Straker's body.	☐	☐
6 John Straker's body was in the stables.	☐	☐
7 Inspector Gregory knows all the answers.	☐	☐
8 Sherlock Holmes goes down to Dartmoor.	☐	☐

2 Some of these things are helpful for finding the answer to the mystery. Can you guess which? Tick nine of the sixteen boxes.

☐ a betting book   ☐ some hair
☐ somebody's dinner   ☐ a horseshoe
☐ somebody's breakfast   ☐ a chicken
☐ a box of matches   ☐ a dog
☐ a woman's shoes   ☐ a cat
☐ a woman's hat   ☐ some sheep
☐ a man's hat   ☐ a knife
☐ a man's shoes   ☐ a letter

44

While Reading

Read Chapters 1 and 2. How much do we know now about the mystery? Which of these sentences are true, and which are possibly true, but we don't really know yet?

1 Someone killed John Straker on Monday night.
2 Silver Blaze disappeared the same night.
3 Silver Blaze is dead.
4 Before Monday, Silver Blaze was the favourite to win the Wessex Cup.
5 Ned Hunter did not take Fitzroy Simpson's money.
6 John Straker found Fitzroy Simpson in the stables in the middle of the night.
7 Fitzroy Simpson put opium in Ned Hunter's curry.
8 Edith Baxter put opium in Ned Hunter's curry.
9 Ned Hunter slept all night because of the opium.
10 Fitzroy Simpson killed John Straker.

Before you read Chapter 3, can you guess what Holmes does next? Choose one answer for each question.

1 Which of these people does Holmes talk to?
   a) Ned Hunter   b) Mrs Straker   c) Fitzroy Simpson
2 What does Holmes find in the mud on the moor?
   a) an envelope   b) a horseshoe   c) a broken match

Read Chapters 3 and 4. We can answer some of these questions now, but not all of them. Answer the questions when you can, and write 'Don't know yet' for the others.

1 Why did Simpson have a ten-pound note in an envelope?
2 Why did John Straker take a doctor's eye knife with him that night?
3 What was the dress-maker's bill for?
4 Why did Mr Darbyshire's letters come to Straker's house?
5 How did Holmes know that the tracks on the moor were Silver Blaze's?
6 What did Silas Brown do to Silver Blaze?
7 Why did Holmes want to go back to London that night?
8 Why wasn't Mr Ross happy with Holmes's promise?
9 Why did Holmes want a photograph of John Straker?
10 What was important about the lame sheep?
11 What did the dog at the stables do in the night-time?
12 Why was that strange?

Before you read Chapter 5 (*A day at the races*), can you guess what happens? Choose one answer for each question.

1 What happens in the Wessex Cup race? Silver Blaze . . .
   a) wins the race.   c) comes last.
   b) comes second.   d) falls and breaks a leg.
2 Who doesn't go to the races?
   a) Sherlock Holmes.   c) Inspector Gregory.
   b) Dr Watson.   d) Mr Ross.

3 Where is John Straker's killer on that day?

   a) In the Dartmoor stables   c) In a police station.

   b) At the races.   d) In London.

Read Chapter 5. Choose the best question-word for these questions, and then answer them.

What / Why

1 . . . was Mr Ross very pleased with Sherlock Holmes?

2 . . . was the name of John Straker's killer?

3 . . . did Holmes want to talk about it later?

How does the story end? Before you read Chapter 6, look at these sentences. Can you guess how many are true? Choose as many as you like.

1 The dog did not bark because it did not hear the midnight visitor.

2 The midnight visitor to the stables was John Straker.

3 John Straker wanted to kill Silver Blaze.

4 John Straker wanted Silver Blaze to win the Wessex Cup.

5 John Straker wanted to win a lot of money on the Wessex Cup race.

6 Straker used the eye knife to cut Silver Blaze's leg.

7 In London Holmes visited a dress-maker.

8 Mr William Darbyshire was a good friend of Straker's.

9 Sherlock Holmes tells Mr Ross all about Silas Brown.

After Reading

1 **Match the names with the sentences. Then use the sentences to write about the people. Use a pronoun (*he*) and linking words (*and, but, so, because*) where possible.**

Mr Ross / Silas Brown / John Straker / Fitzroy Simpson

Example: *Mr Ross wanted Sherlock Holmes to find his horse, but he did not understand detective work and . . .*

1 _____ changed the colour of Silver Blaze's coat.
2 _____ made his money taking bets at the races.
3 _____ needed money for the expensive Mrs Darbyshire.
4 *Mr Ross* wanted Sherlock Holmes to find his horse.
5 _____ went down to King's Pyland stables.
6 _____ tried to make Silver Blaze a little lame.
7 _____ was afraid of the police.
8 *Mr Ross* did not understand detective work.
9 _____ wanted to ask the stable boys some questions.
10 _____ went to the stables in the middle of the night.
11 _____ told Sherlock Holmes everything.
12 _____ took Silver Blaze out onto the moor.
13 _____ wanted answers to the mystery at once.
14 _____ took Silver Blaze to Winchester races.
15 _____ never came home again.

2 Here is a new illustration. Answer the questions, and then find a good place in the story to put the picture.

1 What is happening in this picture?
2 What is *not* happening in this picture?
3 What does the answer to the second question tell us?

A good place for the picture is on page _____.

Now write a caption for the illustration.

Caption: _____

3 **What did Sherlock Holmes say to Silas Brown? Put their conversation in the right order, and write in the speakers' names. Sherlock Holmes speaks first (number 3).**

1 _____ 'A different colour? The police are going to find that very interesting, Mr Brown.'

2 _____ 'And how do you know that?'

3 _____ 'Now, Mr Silas Brown, I want to see Silver Blaze.'

4 _____ 'Yes, I have. He's round the back. He's . . . er . . . well, he's a different colour now.'

5 _____ 'Yes. And he must win it! With your help, Mr Brown. Now, listen carefully, . . .'

6 _____ 'The tracks . . . Oh. Oh dear.'

7 _____ 'My name is Sherlock Holmes, and I *know* that the horse is here.'

8 _____ 'Don't tell the police, sir. Please! I can change the colour back very quickly.'

9 _____ 'Yes, Mr Brown, oh dear! Now, have you got the horse here?'

10 _____ 'Yes, very well. He's a wonderful horse, sir. He can still win the Wessex Cup, you know.'

11 _____ 'Because I found the tracks of your shoes on the moor, next to the tracks of Silver Blaze, and the tracks came here.'

12 _____ 'He's not in my stables! And who are *you*?'

13 _____ 'Then you must do it today. Is the horse well?'

4 Here is a newspaper report about Silver Blaze. Use these words (one for each gap) to complete the passage.

before, bets, cut, disappeared, found, good, horse, horseshoes, kicked, killed, killer, knows, leg, mystery, owner, races, where, won

At Winchester _____ today Silver Blaze _____ the Wessex Cup –_____ news for the _____ Mr Ross and all the people with _____ on the horse. The detective Sherlock Holmes _____ Mr Ross's horse, and he _____ the name of John Straker's _____ too.

So who _____ John Straker? The _____ did! Straker tried to make a _____ in a tendon in Silver Blaze's _____ , and the horse _____ out. The _____ hit Straker on the head and killed him. The horse then _____ until today.

And _____ was Silver Blaze in the week _____ the Wessex Cup race? That is still a _____.

5 Find the fourteen words (three letters or more) in this word search. Words go from left to right, and from top to bottom. Which four words make a headline for the newspaper report?

S	H	E	E	P	W	I	N	N	I	N	G	T	T
C	O	H	Q	L	L	K	I	L	L	E	D	R	A
A	R	F	T	R	A	I	N	E	R	F	B	A	S
R	S	M	U	D	M	K	I	C	K	G	E	C	T
F	E	S	A	F	E	O	W	N	E	R	T	K	E

51

ABOUT THE AUTHOR

Sir Arthur Conan Doyle (1859–1930) was born in Edinburgh, Scotland. He studied medicine and worked as a doctor for eight years. But he needed more money, so he began writing short stories for weekly magazines.

In his first novel, *A Study in Scarlet* (1887), Sherlock Holmes appeared for the first time – a strange, but very clever detective, who smokes a pipe, plays the violin, and lives at 221B Baker Street in London. He can find the answer to almost any problem, and likes to explain how easy it is to his slow-thinking friend, Dr Watson ('Elementary, my dear Watson!'). Sherlock Holmes appeared again in *The Sign of Four* (1890), and short stories about him, in the *Strand* magazine, were very popular.

Conan Doyle himself was more interested in writing novels about history, like *The White Company* (1891), and he became bored with Sherlock Holmes. So, in the short story called *The Final Problem* (1893), he 'killed' him, and Holmes and his famous enemy, Moriarty, fell to their deaths in the Reichenbach falls. But Conan Doyle's readers were very unhappy about this because they wanted more stories about Holmes, so Conan Doyle had to bring Holmes back to life, in *The Hound of the Baskervilles* (1902) – perhaps the most famous of all the Sherlock Holmes stories.

There are more than fifty short stories about Sherlock Holmes. You can read them in almost any language, and there are many plays and films about the great detective.

OXFORD BOOKWORMS LIBRARY

Classics • Crime & Mystery • Factfiles • Fantasy & Horror
Human Interest • Playscripts • Thriller & Adventure
True Stories • World Stories

The OXFORD BOOKWORMS LIBRARY provides enjoyable reading in English, with a wide range of classic and modern fiction, non-fiction, and plays. It includes original and adapted texts in seven carefully graded language stages, which take learners from beginner to advanced level. An overview is given on the next pages.

All Stage 1 titles are available as audio recordings, as well as over eighty other titles from Starter to Stage 6. All Starters and many titles at Stages 1 to 4 are specially recommended for younger learners. Every Bookworm is illustrated, and Starters and Factfiles have full-colour illustrations.

The OXFORD BOOKWORMS LIBRARY also offers extensive support. Each book contains an introduction to the story, notes about the author, a glossary, and activities. Additional resources include tests and worksheets, and answers for these and for the activities in the books. There is advice on running a class library, using audio recordings, and the many ways of using Oxford Bookworms in reading programmes. Resource materials are available on the website <www.oup.com/elt/gradedreaders>.

The *Oxford Bookworms Collection* is a series for advanced learners. It consists of volumes of short stories by well-known authors, both classic and modern. Texts are not abridged or adapted in any way, but carefully selected to be accessible to the advanced student.

You can find details and a full list of titles in the *Oxford Bookworms Library Catalogue* and *Oxford English Language Teaching Catalogues*, and on the website <www.oup.com/elt/gradedreaders>.

THE OXFORD BOOKWORMS LIBRARY
GRADING AND SAMPLE EXTRACTS

STARTER • 250 HEADWORDS

present simple – present continuous – imperative –
can/cannot, must – *going to* (future) – simple gerunds ...

Her phone is ringing – but where is it?

Sally gets out of bed and looks in her bag. No phone. She looks under the bed. No phone. Then she looks behind the door. There is her phone. Sally picks up her phone and answers it. *Sally's Phone*

STAGE 1 • 400 HEADWORDS

... past simple – coordination with *and, but, or* –
subordination with *before, after, when, because, so* ...

I knew him in Persia. He was a famous builder and I worked with him there. For a time I was his friend, but not for long. When he came to Paris, I came after him – I wanted to watch him. He was a very clever, very dangerous man. *The Phantom of the Opera*

STAGE 2 • 700 HEADWORDS

... present perfect – *will* (future) – *(don't) have to, must not, could* –
comparison of adjectives – simple *if* clauses – past continuous –
tag questions – *ask/tell* + infinitive ...

While I was writing these words in my diary, I decided what to do. I must try to escape. I shall try to get down the wall outside. The window is high above the ground, but I have to try. I shall take some of the gold with me – if I escape, perhaps it will be helpful later. *Dracula*

... should, may – present perfect continuous – *used to* – past perfect –
causative – relative clauses – indirect statements ...

Of course, it was most important that no one should see
Colin, Mary, or Dickon entering the secret garden. So Colin
gave orders to the gardeners that they must all keep away
from that part of the garden in future. ***The Secret Garden***

STAGE 4 • 1400 HEADWORDS

... past perfect continuous – passive (simple forms) –
would conditional clauses – indirect questions –
relatives with *where/when* – gerunds after prepositions/phrases ...

I was glad. Now Hyde could not show his face to the world
again. If he did, every honest man in London would be proud
to report him to the police. ***Dr Jekyll and Mr Hyde***

STAGE 5 • 1800 HEADWORDS

... future continuous – future perfect –
passive (modals, continuous forms) –
would have conditional clauses – modals + perfect infinitive ...

If he had spoken Estella's name, I would have hit him. I was so
angry with him, and so depressed about my future, that I could
not eat the breakfast. Instead I went straight to the old house.
Great Expectations

STAGE 6 • 2500 HEADWORDS

... passive (infinitives, gerunds) – advanced modal meanings –
clauses of concession, condition

When I stepped up to the piano, I was confident. It was as if I
knew that the prodigy side of me really did exist. And when I
started to play, I was so caught up in how lovely I looked that I
didn't worry how I would sound. ***The Joy Luck Club***

Sherlock Holmes and the Duke's Son

SIR ARTHUR CONAN DOYLE

Retold by Jennifer Bassett

Dr Huxtable has a school for boys in the north of England. When the Duke of Holdernesse decides to send his young son there, that is good news for the school. The Duke is a very important person, and Dr Huxtable is happy to have his son in the school.

But two weeks later Dr Huxtable is the unhappiest man in England. Why? And why does he take the train down to London and go to Baker Street? Why does he need the help of the famous detective Sherlock Holmes?

Because someone has kidnapped the Duke's son . . .

Sister Love and Other Crime Stories

JOHN ESCOTT

Some sisters are good friends, some are not. Sometimes there is more hate in a family than there is love. Karin is beautiful and has lots of men friends, but she can be very unkind to her sister Marcia. Perhaps when they were small, there was love between them, but that was a long time ago.

They say that everybody has one crime in them. Perhaps they only take an umbrella that does not belong to them. Perhaps they steal from a shop, perhaps they get angry and hit someone, perhaps they kill . . .